tECHiES

Shawn Fanning

Shawn Fanning

[Napster and the Music Revolution]

0400454

✳

CHRISTOPHER MITTEN

TWENTY-FIRST CENTURY BOOKS
BROOKFIELD, CONNECTICUT

Special thanks to Seth Meyers for contributing "Tech Talk"
Design by Lynne Amft

Produced by 17th Street Productions,
an Alloy, Inc. company
151 West 26th Street, New York, NY 10001

Library of Congress Cataloging-in-Publication Data

Mitten, Christopher
Shawn Fanning : Napster and the music revolution / by Christopher Mitten.
    p. cm.—(Techies)
Summary: A biography of the founder and director of the music exchange internet company,
Napster, focusing on the court cases of 2000.
ISBN 0-7613-2656-1 (lib. bdg.)
1. Fanning, Shawn—Juvenile literature. 2. Napster, Inc.—Juvenile literature. 3. Computer
networks—United States—Biography—Juvenile literature. 4. Peer-to-peer architecture
(Computer networks)—Juvenile literature. 5. Sound—Recording and reproducing—Digital
techniques—Computer network resources—Juvenile literature. 6. Music trade—Juvenile
literature. [1. Fanning, Shawn. 2. Napster, Inc. 3. Businesspeople. 4. Computer networks.
5. Sound—Recording and reproducing—Digital techniques. 6. Music trade.] I. Title: Napster
and the music revolution. II. Title. III. Series.

TK5102.56.F35 M57 2002
025.06'78'092—dc21
[B]   2001049168

contents

CHAPTER ONE

A New Kind of Internet

An Afternoon with the Senate

ON OCTOBER 9, 2000, A BROAD-SHOULDERED, CONFIDENT KID, JUST NINETEEN YEARS OLD, TOOK A SEAT BEFORE THE UNITED STATES SENATE JUDICIARY COMMITTEE. HIS NAME WAS SHAWN FANNING, AND HE HAD BEEN HAVING A STRANGE YEAR. IN A MATTER OF MONTHS HE HAD REVOLUTIONIZED THE WORLD WIDE WEB, STARTED A COMPANY WORTH MIL-LIONS OF DOLLARS, PROVOKED ONE OF THE LARGEST LAW-SUITS IN THE HISTORY OF THE MUSIC INDUSTRY, AND—TO TOP IT ALL OFF—CAUSED ONE OF HIS FAVORITE BANDS,

Metallica, to denounce him as a thief. He was now being called to explain himself. And not just to anyone. He was before one of the most powerful legal institutions in the world.

The hearings were held in Provo, Utah, the home of Senator Orrin Hatch, the Judiciary Committee's chairman. Hatch's opinions would have a big impact on Shawn Fanning's future, and, unfortunately, the senator was not known as a gentle and easygoing man. To make matters worse, everyone on the Judiciary Committee was at least a generation older than Fanning. Few committee members understood the nature of his company, known as Napster. Few even had a decent grasp of the Internet. They did understand, however, that Fanning had been causing quite a stir.

Fanning was the author of a seemingly simple computer program that allowed people to share music over the Internet. His program and his company had raised a major challenge to the twenty-billion-dollar-per-year music business. Music that cost seventeen dollars per compact disc was now being exchanged for free on Napster. Record companies, business executives, and musicians were furious.

At the time of the Senate hearings, the U.S. courts were in the process of deciding on the fate of Fanning's company. But many critics were saying that the debate over Napster was too important to leave to the discretion of judges. They were calling for congressional action. The hearings were being held to decide if this was appropriate.

But despite the fury of the record industry, the power of the Judiciary Committee, and the magnitude of the stakes, Fanning had a lot going for him. Record executives might hate him, but the thirty million users of Napster saw him as a hero. It was not out of the question that by the end of the hearings he could win over a few senators. Fanning had been defending his work for more than a year. He had been thinking about the possibilities and future of the Internet for much longer. He had, in fact, come to represent the generation of young people who had grown up with the Web. There were members on the committee who were very interested in his point of view. And they wanted to hear the story behind the founding of Napster.

Shawn Fanning grew up in Harwich, Massachusetts, on the southern shore of Cape Cod. He was a pretty ordinary kid, although by the time he was a sophomore in high school, he was beginning to distinguish himself as an excellent student and an excellent athlete. Still, few would have predicted that by nineteen he would be one of the most talked-about people in the United States. His most distinctive feature seemed to be his curly hair, which was usually matted down because he always wore a baseball cap. His hair even earned him a special nickname—The Napster—because it was always a mess, or "nappy."

The seaside town of Harwich, where Shawn Fanning grew up

If you asked Shawn what he liked to do in those days, he would have told you that he liked to work out, listen to music, hang out with friends, and everything else you'd expect a fifteen year old to enjoy. But in 1996, the summer after his sophomore year, all that changed. That summer Shawn's uncle, John Fanning, bought him a computer and hooked him up to the Internet.

Shawn took to the computer instantly. He immediately started learning programming languages and surfing the Web. His uncle even got him his own phone line so he didn't have to compete with his parents or his four siblings for the phone. Slowly his computer began to take up more and more

Shawn Fanning

of his time. He spent hours visiting chat rooms (where he used "Napster" as his screen name), checking out new sites, and playing video games—his uncle, in fact, owned a software company called NetGames that developed games for the Internet. Soon Shawn's interest in computers and programming blocked out everything else. He gave up sports (though not his workouts at the gym) and devoted himself entirely to his new passion.

Still, Shawn was no computer geek. In fact, just the opposite. He started bringing in extra cash through a part-time job at his uncle's company in Hull, Massachusetts, not far from his home. As a bonus, he was allowed to use a company car, which just happened to be a BMW Z3. Sure, Fanning was known around school as that kid with the messy hair who loved computers. But he was also known as the guy with the coolest car in school.

Along with the car and the job, John Fanning also gave his nephew lots of advice. He was Shawn's mentor and did his best to take care of him. Shawn had not had an easy life when he was younger. He had never known his biological father. He was close to his stepfather, but a temporary split between his mother and stepfather had led Shawn and his siblings to live briefly in a foster home. And money was tight. The family wasn't exactly poor, but there were five children to take care of and not a lot of extra money to go around.

Shawn's uncle (his mother's brother) watched over him. He offered Shawn guidance and even bribed him to achieve in school—Shawn got a hundred dollars for every A on his report card. More important, John Fanning showed his nephew that life could be pretty sweet if you set goals and did the work necessary to achieve them. It was a lesson that would soon lead to a big payoff for Shawn.

The other good thing about Shawn's close relationship with his uncle was that he was exposed to lots of computer programmers. John Fanning's company employed college students and recent college grads to write code—the thousands of instructions that make up a computer program. Shawn Fanning learned the tricks of the trade from these older kids. He also determined that his time in college would be spent pursuing a degree in computer science. He was, after all, programming right alongside people who were taking or had even finished college courses in programming. It would be a natural fit.

In fact, Fanning was so well prepared for a degree in computer science that in the fall of 1999, when he arrived as a freshman at Northeastern University in Boston—just about 50 miles (80 kilometers) north of Harwich—he was immediately placed in junior- and senior-level courses. Without question, he was a kid who could go far in college. However, it was not to be. By the middle of Fanning's freshman year, he had become absorbed in a particular computing problem. He was so absorbed that he would soon drop out of college to pursue it.

Shawn Fanning's uncle John was a little worried about Shawn's progress in college. The issue was not whether he could do the work. It was just that Fanning seemed to spend more of his time hanging around his uncle's company than at Northeastern. John Fanning was concerned about Shawn's lack of motivation.

In many ways, Shawn Fanning wasn't really cut out for college. He was smart enough and self-motivated enough that he had already learned many of the things his professors were teaching. So he was just a bit bored. He had already worked for a real software developer. He had already had the chance to create and improve real programs. College didn't quite have the same challenge or demand the same focus.

One of the things that did absorb Shawn's interest was music and the exchange of MP3 files over the Internet. An MP3 file (or MPEG Audio Layer 3) provides a way that songs can be exchanged across the World Wide Web. It takes digitally recorded music from a CD, stores it on a hard drive, and plays it through a special computer program. Shawn Fanning and his roommates at Northeastern loved music. And with MP3 technology, they could get almost any song they wanted for free. They just had to locate it on the Internet.

That, however, could be a problem. As amazing as the Internet was, it could also be unreliable. Finding a song could take forever using standard search engines. The problem had to do with something called indexing. When you use a search engine on the Web, say Yahoo! or Lycos, you're using a kind of index. The index is a huge record of all the things on the Internet. You can search the index by typing key words into the entry field. The problem is that these indexes aren't always up-to-date. Links can lead nowhere. Web pages are often down. Or the page is working, but what you are searching for is missing. What Shawn Fanning and his roommates found so frustrating was that they

Northeastern University, where Shawn Fanning studied before he left to found Napster

would follow link after link looking for a song, only to be disappointed by error codes and missing pages on sites that had been shut down or simply weren't kept up-to-date. If the problem was to be solved, a new means of indexing had to be found.

But as with many things in life, the difficulty of finding MP3s just seemed to be an inevitable problem. It was the way the Web worked. It wasn't ideal, but what could anyone do? For Shawn's roommates the slow transfer of MP3s was just an annoying thing to complain about. For Shawn, however, it was a problem to be solved. That problem would eventually lead to months of obsessive research and programming, and ultimately to the birth of Napster.

A New Obsession

When coders talk shop, they say that there are a few characteristics that set the great programmers apart from the merely good ones. The ability to obsess over an idea, to completely focus on it, is at the top of the list. When a programmer begins to focus on his or her code, it means eighteen-hour days, a diet of pizza and soda, and little contact with friends except for the people you bump into in online chat rooms when you're looking for some help with your program.

At first the problem of how to best find MP3s on the Internet was not an obsession for Shawn Fanning. It was more like a hobby. He worked on it occasionally, maybe after playing hoops at the gym or while he was eating dinner. The work went in spurts. It did not consume him entirely.

Part of the reason for this was that an effective MP3 program required him to learn a new way of programming. He was used to programming for an operating system called UNIX, favored by technically sophisticated users. But most nontechnical people use the Microsoft Windows operating system; if Shawn wanted to swap MP3 files with lots of people, he needed to write a program for the operating system that most people use. So Shawn experimented with the new operating system. But he had a lot to learn.

Still, Fanning had approached new and difficult problems before. It wasn't hard for him to figure out how to program for the Windows operating system. And after a while his program became more than a hobby. As he told the Senate Judiciary Committee in the fall of 2000, "I very quickly became totally absorbed in this project. It was more compelling than my classes and more meaningful than socializing at school."

Fanning's uncle also noticed the change. It occurred to him that Shawn's project might not be the best thing for his grades. But Fanning was so engrossed in his work that his uncle decided it could only be a good thing. Fanning's uncle was a programmer himself. He knew what it meant when that kind of focus set in. It meant that Fanning was probably onto something good. And even if it was a disaster, the experience of putting together a major program would teach him a lot.

The Birth of Peer-to-Peer File Sharing

So what exactly was the solution that began to obsess Fanning? It's now known as peer-to-peer (or P2P) file sharing. It was a whole new way of thinking about how to use the Internet. Eventually it would revolutionize the way music was passed around the Web. More important, it would forever alter the way all applications on the Internet would be written.

In the case of music, peer-to-peer file sharing basically means that people looking for and collecting MP3 files can open up their hard drives and share their MP3s with others doing the same thing. So, rather than having centralized Web sites from which users download music, a peer-to-peer system depends on a decentralized wealth of personal computers to store and share the files. The computer program and Web site that Fanning imagined would help MP3 collectors find each other and exchange MP3s. This Web site would not, however, store the actual MP3s. Fanning's program was a new method of indexing—one that would be very effective in locating the MP3s that were nearly impossible to find on the indexes built by traditional search engines.

Shawn Fanning understood that there were also other benefits to peer-to-peer systems. First, if there was a centralized indexing site, it would be easier to spread the word about unknown or underappreciated musicians. With a centralized index of MP3s you could develop communities of people with similar interests. One person could sign into a chat room, hear about a great new singer, and then download a song from the same site. Shawn himself was a guitar player and even thought that Napster might be a good way to spread his own music.

The bigger issue, and the one that led both to Napster's fame and to the colossal lawsuits that followed, was that it theoretically allowed people to swap MP3 files without infringing on copyright laws. It was generally illegal to store and distribute MP3s on the Web because of copyright violations—songs were being downloaded and played, but record companies weren't getting paid. This is one of the reasons MP3s had been so hard to find. They were usually stored on small sites that were constantly being moved or changed.

A person is not allowed to duplicate copyrighted material for profit or in bulk. But a person can record songs from an album and pass them along to a friend. For instance, making a mixed tape for a buddy or a boyfriend is perfectly legal. What Napster and its peer-to-peer site did was to make possible the large-scale exchange of copyrighted music without actually distributing the music itself. Napster was never once in possession of any of the songs. The songs themselves were on people's private hard drives. Napster did two things: one, it stored an index of all the MP3s on the hard drives of all the registered Napster users, and two, it transferred MP3s among Napster users.

This promised to avoid a huge legal problem. If Napster were a site where music was given out for free, it would have been shut down instantly. But in Shawn Fanning's understanding—and this was an argument he would repeat over and over before too long—peer-to-peer file swapping simply enables the same kind of sharing that happens when people make mixed tapes for each other. And that was why the whole thing was legal.

But these issues were still months away. In the fall of 1999, when Shawn Fanning was mulling over programming problems in his dorm room, Napster, the company, did not exist yet. All the same, the project was gaining momentum. Shawn had come up with a great idea, and he had started to do the work necessary to make his idea a reality.

Now Shawn had some hard choices to make. He might be able to write his program and continue his college education. But the chances were that both projects would suffer. Dropping out of school was a way to focus on his ideas for a peer-to-peer network. On the other hand, dropping out of school seemed like a pretty crazy move. How far would he be able to get in life without a college degree?

At seventeen, Shawn Fanning was already facing the biggest decision of his life.

CHAPTER TWO

The Dropout

A Trip Back to Hull

SHAWN FANNING SUCCESSFULLY COMPLETED HIS FIRST SEM-
ESTER AT NORTHEASTERN. HIS PROJECT OF CREATING A FILE-
SWAPPING PROGRAM WAS NOW IN FULL SWING. IT WAS STILL A
MESS. THERE WERE PLENTY OF BUGS IN THE CODE. BUT THE
PROGRAM (WHICH HE WAS ALREADY CALLING NAPSTER) WAS
IMPROVING. FANNING WAS MOVING FORWARD. AND HIS
OBSESSION CONTINUED TO GROW.

HE SPENT MOST OF WINTER BREAK TYPING AWAY ON HIS
LAPTOP COMPUTER, A SOUPED-UP DELL THAT HIS UNCLE HAD

bought him. It soon became Shawn's best friend. He was putting in long hours, often sprawled on the floor of his uncle's office. He lived on a diet of pizza and cereal—if he ate at all. When he slept, it was usually on the sofa, after marathon programming sessions that ended around dawn. This was not how most college freshmen spent their vacations.

When winter break ended, Shawn returned to Northeastern. But his heart wasn't in it. He headed to Hull for a weekend early in the semester to work on Napster in his uncle's office. His cousin drove him back to Boston for the start of the new week, but by this point Fanning was completely gripped by the idea of completing the program.

Shawn hadn't quite been able to leave school to pursue the project. He knew his mom and stepfather would be upset, and he himself wasn't actually convinced that leaving school after just one semester was a good idea. But when he and his cousin pulled up to his dorm that evening, something snapped. Shawn opened the door, walked a few paces, and then halted. He paused, turned around, and stepped back into his cousin's car. He wasn't going back. His cousin didn't give him a hard time. He just turned the car around and headed back to the NetGames office in Hull.

Shawn Fanning never even went back to pick up his stuff. Mostly he was afraid of bumping into his friends. He said later, in an interview with Northeastern University's student newspaper: "I knew that if I spoke to my suite mates and told them I was making this decision . . . they would question [it]. I knew that I didn't really understand the idea well enough to articulate it to them. I was afraid they wouldn't understand and that they would convince me not to do it."

Avoiding his parents' opinions would not be so easy. Looking back on the decision, it's hard to imagine Fanning doing anything else. The choice between being the kid who changed the Internet and just another college freshman seems like a no-brainer. But at the time, Fanning was taking a big risk. From his parents' point of view, in fact, he was out of his mind.

Today his mother and stepfather couldn't be prouder. But back then, it seemed to them that their son was throwing away a great opportunity. Still, Fanning was determined to finish Napster. It was almost as if he didn't have a choice in the matter. He was so completely devoted to his vision of peer-to-peer music sharing that going back to school was simply impossible.

Maybe because he was a programmer himself, Shawn's uncle John found it easier to accept. Before long Shawn was back on the floor of his uncle's office, spending time with his laptop and puzzling over how to bring his ideas to life.

Doubters, Cynics, and Naysayers

One of the secrets to Shawn Fanning's success is his resourcefulness. He understood that in some ways, he was working at a disadvantage. He was learning operating systems on the fly, he was still developing his skills with the systems he knew, and he had never really written a program of Napster's size and scope. But Fanning had lots of friends in the business, and he wasn't afraid to ask questions. He also had contacts all over the world through the relationships he had developed in online chat rooms. When he got stuck, it didn't take long for him to find someone who could help him out. In fact, it was in a chat room that Fanning met two of Napster's future programmers: Jordan Ritter and Sean Parker.

The drawback to Fanning's resourcefulness was that it also opened him up to criticism. There were plenty of people who wanted to tell him that his idea wouldn't work. It wasn't just an issue of writing the program. An even bigger potential stumbling block was the fact that the Napster software depended on people being willing to open up their hard drives to strangers. That kind of sharing is the essence of a peer-to-peer network. The more cynical voices said that no one would be willing to participate in such an open community. Fortunately Fanning didn't pay much attention to this criticism. And his hunch that people would have no problem letting others download files from their personal computers was dead right. Peaking at nearly sixty million users, Napster would eventually prove that people are much more trusting and generous than the cynics believed.

Another issue was legality. The music industry was now doing everything it could to prevent copies of songs from flowing freely on the Internet. It was harder than ever to locate the songs you wanted. Fanning's program also addressed this problem. Unlike Web sites that posted MP3 files on their server and then uploaded them to other computers, Napster would never be in possession of or distribute the music. It simply indexed files on different people's hard drives. It wasn't handing out free copies of copyrighted music. It was just making it easier for one person to share songs with another. It was like an enormous, communal mixed tape, one that was fully digitized and contained almost every song ever recorded.

Of course, the people who warned Fanning about the legal implications of his program were onto something. But by the time the music industry had taken Napster to court—only one year after Fanning had made the decision not to return to Northeastern University—the revolution had already occurred. The music industry would have its legal victories. But after Napster there would be no going back, no matter what happened in court.

A "Killer Application" That Would Change the Internet

So Shawn Fanning had his critics and doubters. But his confidence and his talent far outweighed any of the potential negatives. This won him plenty of supporters. The most important of these continued to be his uncle. John Fanning understood what it took to produce a great program. He didn't find it at all strange to show up for work every morning in the spring of 1999 to find his nephew hunched over his laptop with empty pizza boxes and Coke cans strewn around him. That was what it took to write great code. And since John had never seen his nephew so taken with an idea, he was willing to give Shawn all the space he needed.

Shawn also believed in himself. He loved to compete, and the more people expressed doubts about Napster, the more he wanted to prove it would work. He was also consumed with another notion. He was convinced that there were other people working on the same idea. It made so much sense to him that it was hard to imagine that others were not also developing peer-to-peer software. In fact, Fanning was way ahead of his time. But he didn't know this, and the idea that he might be beaten to the punch kept him glued to his computer.

At this point, being first was more a matter of honor than a business proposition. Shawn knew he had a lot to gain with Napster. But he also figured that even if he was first to develop

P2P MP3 software, the idea would be adopted by more established businesses and that his glory would mostly lie with other programmers. He had no idea that sixty million people would soon be using his software on a daily basis.

Fortunately Fanning's uncle also helped him out in this regard. Shawn was a kid in love with computers. He was also a visionary—he saw the Internet being used in a way that hadn't even crossed anyone else's mind. His uncle had some of these qualities as well, but his uncle was first and foremost a businessman. He knew how to take a good program and bring it to life in the real world. He also knew the legal steps required to build a company. And he had great contacts in the business community. That meant investors, and investors meant money.

And fortunately for Shawn, his uncle had developed one other thing while he was watching his nephew sprawled on the floor, tapping away at his Dell. Shawn's uncle developed the unswerving belief that Shawn was not just making a cool application for his buddies in the dorm; he had begun to understand that Shawn was onto something that could change the world.

TECH TALK

MP3 digital music format

On the backs of such music-sharing Internet sites as Napster, MP3 audio has swept the music-listening public with unprecedented speed. There are now MP3 players for your computer, MP3-format Walkmen, MP3 programs for personal data assistants (like PalmPilot), MP3-playing cell phones, even a wristwatch that plays MP3s.

But what exactly is MP3?

MP3 is short for MPEG Audio Layer 3. MPEG refers to the Moving Pictures Experts Group, an organization that sets international standards for digital formats for audio and video. MP3 is a codec, or compression/decompression algorithm. It's a software formula designed to take music and store it in as small a file as possible while still preserving a very high level of quality.

The need for MP3 became apparent with the widespread desire to share and download audio over the Internet. Most people have Internet connections that aren't very well suited to transferring conventional CD-quality music. The typical 56-K modem would take about a half hour to download the ten megabytes of data that make up just a minute of CD-quality audio. A song might take two hours to download. And forget about the thirty hours or so that you would need for an entire CD!

MP3 became popular because it could reduce the ten megabytes or so that make up a minute of music by a factor of ten or more. With MP3 you can get the same minute's worth of music in only about one megabyte of data. Now you can

download that four-minute song in about twelve minutes instead of two hours. That's a big improvement.

MP3 is a "perceptual" codec—it works on the principle that there are certain categories of sounds that humans can't perceive and that these can safely be thrown away without diminishing the basic quality of the recording. This kind of compression is called "lossy" because some of the data get lost and can never be restored.

Examples of this extraneous data include very high sounds—frequencies above about twenty kilohertz. You can't hear them (though your dog can). MP3 eliminates these very high sounds and some very low ones, too. It cuts out very soft sounds when they are playing at the same time as very loud ones. You can't hear them, anyway, so why keep them? If it finds two notes that are very similar, it merges them into one sound. It's a process that involves compromise: throw away too much audio and you will hear the difference; throw away too little and your file will still be too big.

After throwing out the parts of your music that you probably won't miss, MP3 then uses "lossless" compression to make the file even smaller without losing any more data. It looks for patterns or repetitions in the audio signal that can be represented by a kind of shorthand. For example, if there is a two-second silence, rather than storing the thirty-two thousand bytes necessary to say "silence" over and over for two seconds, MP3 uses just two bytes: one to say "silence" and one to say "repeat thirty-two thousand times." The same would hold true for a trumpet note or a backup singer's riff: the MP3 codec looks for stretches of data that

repeat themselves and tries to save them only once. The result is a much smaller file.

The process of making an MP3 file:

1. First you copy a song off an audio CD onto your computer's hard drive. This process is called "ripping," and the result is usually a .wav file, identical in size and quality to the original CD audio track and ready for encoding.

2. Next you encode the wave file. This means you use a program that has the MP3 codec to compress the .wav file, resulting in a much smaller MP3 file.

MP3 was revolutionary because of its ability to retain high audio quality in a small file size. But programmers never rest, and MP3Pro is on the horizon. It promises to deliver the same high quality at half the size of MP3 by splitting the source audio into two pieces, a high frequency and a low frequency, and compressing them separately. By splitting up the sound like this, the MP3Pro codec can do an even more efficient job on each half, resulting in an even smaller file.

CHAPTER THREE

From Cape Cod to Silicon Valley

The Company Man

FOR THAT WHOLE SPRING FANNING CONTINUED TO WORK ON NAPSTER. THE MORE PROGRESS HE MADE, THE HARDER HE WORKED. THE END WAS NOW IN SIGHT. HE KNEW THAT HE COULD MAKE THE SOFTWARE WORK. AND BECAUSE HE KNEW THE SOFTWARE WOULD WORK, HE BEGAN TO UNDERSTAND JUST HOW BIG THIS PROGRAM COULD BE.

IN MANY WAYS SHAWN FANNING IS A LOW-KEY GUY. HE'S KNOWN AMONG THE PRESS CORPS FOR HIS SHYNESS AND MODESTY. IN INTERVIEWS TODAY HE'S THE FIRST TO TELL YOU that he's still in a state of disbelief over what's happened to him over the previous two years. And even as his code was falling into place that spring, he wondered if he were crazy. But he also had a vision, and whatever doubts he had, he also saw the enormous potential of the project he had embarked on.

Shawn's uncle had come to fully believe in Napster, too, and his relationship with his nephew altered slightly. He was still Shawn's friend, supporter, and mentor. But he added a new component to their interactions. He became Shawn's business partner. John Fanning knew that Napster could become a great business. Perhaps it would eventually charge a small user fee. Perhaps they could sell advertising space. One way or another, it was clear to John Fanning that Napster had great potential.

In May 1999, a month before Shawn completed the first working version of his software, John Fanning incorporated Napster. It was now a company registered with the government. It had legal and economic status, and Shawn and John could interact with the business world as a business, not just as a proud uncle and a college kid with a good idea. John Fanning had already talked to people in the music and Internet businesses. More important, he spoke to lawyers who had significant experience dealing with music copyrights. The music industry had spent a significant amount of time shutting down Web sites that actually had possession of and posted MP3s. They had also spent a lot of money suing companies that manufactured MP3 players. John Fanning talked to people who had been part of these cases about the possible legal challenges Napster might face. He understood that the music industry was going after anyone they perceived to be a threat to their twenty-billion-dollar-a-year business. Shawn and his uncle were confident they weren't breaking any laws or infringing on any copyrights. But the music industry was almost sure to have a different view. The Napster team needed to be prepared.

Still, the preliminary legal research and the ultimate incorporation of Napster in May 1999 were both tiny steps. Shawn Fanning hadn't finished the software yet. However confident the Fannings were about Napster, at that point everything was just speculation. New companies fail all the time, even when they're founded on solid ideas. Napster had a lot going for it. But there was no way yet of knowing just how it would perform.

By the end of May, Shawn had finally completed a working version of Napster, which, in programming lingo, is known as a beta version. The software still had bugs, but the best way of finding them was to let people test-drive the program and report their problems. This was the purpose of the beta stage.

On June 1, 1999, Fanning released copies of the Napster software to thirty friends—guys he knew from home, from college, and from his Internet chats. His only requests were that his friends give him feedback and that they not tell anyone else about the program or the site. In a few days nearly four thousand copies of the program had been downloaded from Napster's Web page. His friends were so blown away by Napster, they couldn't keep their promises. They had to tell others about it. Soon Napster was busy indexing hard drives and shooting MP3s from one computer to another. And it kept adding more members.

For Shawn and his uncle, all this was incredible news. They didn't care that the thirty friends had broken their promise. If thousands of people were using Napster that quickly, they knew they had created a winner. All the optimism was now justified. Here was proof that Napster was something people wanted.

Cash Infusions

Raising money for a new business is tough work. You may have confidence in your new idea, but convincing other people to give you their hard-earned cash is a different story. It's especially difficult when the primary business partner is a nineteen-year-old college dropout. But show up with the names of thousands of users and you have a very different story. Investing in the Internet was already the hottest trend in the new economy. And what could be a more exciting and potentially profitable use of the Internet than trading music?

The membership base of Napster was also growing like crazy. In Internet terms, it was expanding virally. Without Fanning or his uncle doing a thing to market the program, people were downloading and passing it along on their own. It spread like a virus, from one person to the next. This is tempting information to a potential investor. When something spreads that quickly just by reputation and word of mouth, you know it's something people really want.

John Fanning took the membership numbers and basic information about Napster to his contacts. He went to friends, former business partners, and various venture capitalists who had money to invest in a new company. He also worked with high-tech businesspeople, marketing experts, and Web site developers. Eventually he found two important partners. One was Yosi Amram, an MBA from Harvard and one of John Fanning's personal friends. The other was John Bales, who was an experienced high-tech entrepreneur. These men put up cash to fund Napster. This in turn helped lend credibility to the project so more people would invest. By the end of the summer John Fanning had raised enough money to fund Napster into the winter. He had also convinced John Bales to join the management team, hiring him as vice president for business development. John Fanning had found the capital to build Napster into a real company. They needed office space, a team of programmers to help Shawn improve Napster, and finance people to continue to raise money and to manage budgets. And they'd need a new chief executive officer—someone who knew the business side of things even better than John Fanning. Someone who could take Napster to the next level.

Sunny San Mateo

The first step was simple. Need new office space for a dot-com start-up? Head to California. By September, Fanning had been installed in an office in San Mateo, in the heart of California's Silicon Valley. The office space was cramped—it was just a couple of rooms above an old bank—but it was better than a small corner in the NetGames headquarters in Hull.

Along with Fanning came other programmers. Many of the key members of his programming team had helped him early on with figuring out problems with Napster's beta version. One of these programmers was Sean Parker. His help was so essential that he's considered by Fanning and others to be one of Napster's cofounders. Parker was also one of Fanning's closest friends. After staying in a hotel for the first few months they eventually moved into a two-bedroom apartment near Napster's offices and resumed pretty much the life that Fanning used to live in the dorm at Northeastern. They bought a wide-screen TV, continued to live on pizza and cereal, downloaded plenty of MP3s, and pulled lots of all-nighters working on code.

The one other important addition to the Napster team was a woman named Eileen Richardson. She was a venture capitalist from Boston whom John Bales had recommended. Shawn and John Fanning thought that

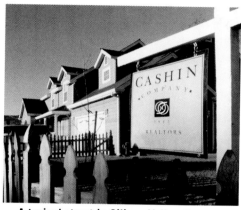

A typical street in Silicon Valley, the new home of Napster, Inc.

Richardson could bring excellent business experience to the table. It would be her job to oversee the transition of Napster from Shawn's pet project into a bona fide company. By anyone's estimation, it would be a huge job. Still, no one had any idea of what was in store for Richardson, the Fannings, and the rest of Napster.

Looking Ahead

All things considered, Napster was roaring ahead. Given the monumental barriers that stand in the way of all new busi-nesses, Napster was a stunning success. Less than a year before, Fanning had been starting his first semester in college. Half a year earlier, he'd been camped out on the floor of his uncle's office. Suddenly he was a business owner, author of a potentially revolutionary piece of software, and having meet-ings with some of the most important financiers and execu-tives in the world. What's more, Napster now had fifteen employees. Fanning was no longer the lone programmer.

Still, Fanning's future was far from certain. He was no longer the smart kid from Harwich who liked computers. He was playing with the pros now. His offices were next to the offices of hundreds of other boy wonders, all praised for their gigantic brains and revolutionary visions. Fanning was com-peting in a brand-new league. All the same, Napster seemed to move to a better position every day. One by one any doubts that people had about Napster's future fell away. But as its success grew, Napster developed new sets of problems.

CHAPTER FOUR

Big Business

The Bandwidth Killer

FANNING UNDERSTOOD THAT HE WAS IN FOR A WILD RIDE WHEN HE ARRIVED IN SAN MATEO. NEVERTHELESS, HE COULD NEVER HAVE PREDICTED HOW MUCH HIS LIFE WOULD CHANGE THAT FALL OF 1999. MOVING TO CALIFORNIA AND STARTING WORK IN NEW OFFICES WAS ENOUGH TO CAUSE FANNING TO HAVE TO MAKE SOME MAJOR READJUSTMENTS. IT WAS QUITE A DIFFERENT WORLD FROM HIS SOLITARY LIFE AT THE NETGAMES OFFICE IN HULL. BUT WHAT HE WOULD BEGIN TO EXPERIENCE AFTER THAT FIRST SEPTEMBER IN SILICON

Valley would become much, much stranger.

First of all, Napster's incubation period came to a sudden and dramatic end. The Napster software was updated and, combined with the growth in membership the company had already been experiencing, Napster's traffic suddenly started booming. By October, Napster was no longer a promising young company. It was a full-fledged phenomenon. Everyone was suddenly monitoring Fanning and his exploding new business.

The main indication of Napster's new strength, aside from the thousands and thousands of people who were downloading it, was the huge amount of bandwidth Napster was taking up on college campuses. Bandwidth is a term that refers to how much information can travel across Internet lines. All servers have a finite amount of bandwidth, although college servers normally have very large bandwidth capacities. Napster, however, was practically shutting down college networks because so many people were using it to trade music. The sheer number of people swapping MP3 files was blocking out all the other Internet traffic. Major universities like the University of Oregon and the University of Florida—

schools with huge computer networks—began to complain that Napster was gobbling up anywhere from 10 to 30 percent of their bandwidth. The University of Illinois at Urbana-Champagne (the birthplace of Netscape) said that at one time it was losing 80 percent of its capacity. Some college networks were so tangled up by Napster that they had to ban the program altogether. It was nothing personal. The Napster site was just too popular, and the college computer systems couldn't keep up.

In the end, more than 130 colleges and universities ended up yanking Napster from their servers. Coders at these institutions programmed their servers to deny students access to Napster's Web site. This wasn't good for membership numbers, but in a sense it was a vindication of Shawn Fanning's initial dream. He and his buddies at Northeastern had been frustrated because they couldn't get hold of the MP3s they wanted. Obviously there were other kids who also wanted to be able to find an easier way to download music. Now millions of college kids were staying up late at night, sampling music, and passing on reviews to their friends, all thanks to a program called Napster.

College students and twenty-somethings are among the most desirable target audience in the world for many companies. College kids spend lots of money, and they set many of the trends that the rest of the world follows. When Napster began commanding the kind of college-age audience that could shut down computer networks, the company started getting lots of attention. And so did Shawn Fanning. Suddenly his story was being told in newspapers and on television around the country. He became a kind of hero for kids on college campuses. People could now share music at the click of a button. It was incredibly easy. And it was free. The guy who created that had to be cool.

All this attention was great for the purpose of finding more investors. But it brought heavy retaliation from the record industries. Why? They felt that every song that was downloaded for free over Napster was a song on which they were losing money through copyright violations. And they had a point. Why would people continue to buy compact discs if they could get music for free online? As great as free music is, there were serious ethical considerations as well. A copyright is a form of property. Record companies make huge investments in acquiring and developing these properties. Musicians and songwriters are also copyright owners, and the royalties they earn based on these copyrights are often an important source of their income. Was it fair to give away all that hard work for free?

The record companies, in conjunction with an organization called the Recording Industry Association of America (or RIAA), quickly entered into negotiations with Napster. They wanted to strike a deal or shut Napster down. But by mid-fall 1999, Napster felt it was in a strong negotiating position and would not be bullied by record executives. A music revolution was happening, and Shawn Fanning's Napster was leading the way. The RIAA claimed that Napster was in clear violation of copyright law. But Shawn Fanning, his uncle, Eileen Richardson, and Napster's lawyers felt that no laws were being broken and that the record companies were in no position to make any demands.

Today many people speculate that the RIAA was, in fact, in a tough position. And they suggest that the RIAA might have

**Hilary Rosen, president of the RIAA, discussing her
organization's lawsuit against Napster**

been willing to offer Napster a deal. If Napster restructured itself and charged users a fee that would be split between record companies and the Web site, both sides of the dispute would have come out ahead. Napster would be making money at last, and the record industry wouldn't be losing as much as it had been. But critics say that the problem was Eileen Richardson and her forceful, tough-as-nails negotiating strategy. The RIAA negotiators were infuriated by the arrogance they felt Richardson and Napster were demonstrating. It made them want to fight rather than negotiate.

It's hard to say whether the criticisms of Richardson are accurate. But the fact remains that Napster wasn't ready to make any deals with an industry that they were suddenly beginning to dominate. The RIAA's reaction? The association had little choice. From their perspective, it was fight or die. So they took the band of rebels to court. On December 7, 1999, just a year after Fanning dropped out of Northeastern, the RIAA and eighteen separate record companies filed suit against Napster for deliberate and widespread copyright violations. They wanted one hundred thousand dollars for every song downloaded. And they wanted Napster shut down. If the RIAA won, Napster would be ruined.

If the RIAA lost? The possibility had everyone shaking in their boots. Other industries understood very well that the RIAA was not alone in all this. Movie studios and book publishers knew that as technology continued to move forward, their products would be the next target of P2P Internet software. How long before Napster would be using its P2P technology to share the latest Wesley Snipes video or the newest Stephen King novel? Most media executives didn't even want to think about it.

The recording industry is a diverse group of people. It is made up not only of high-powered producers and executives; it also includes singers, backup guitarists, songwriters, boy bands, girl bands, orchestra conductors, tuba players, and everyone else whose work has ever gone into the production of a recording. The RIAA represented the industry as a whole. But in terms of specific reactions, musicians responded to Napster in a multitude of ways.

Many artists loved it. Some of them had been scorned by the major record labels and wanted a new way to spread their work. Others were big successes but were tired of seeing other talented musicians struggle to get a break. Napster provided the single best way for a new artist to get exposure. It wasn't just that Napster made the artists' MP3s readily available. It was also that Napster had created a community of music lovers—true to Fanning's dream. When users logged on to Napster, they could enter chat rooms, find out what other people were listening to, read reviews of songs, and even hear from the artists themselves. If a user downloaded a song by

Creed, a list might pop up suggesting other music that user might like, including songs that weren't getting the same kind of support from the so-called music industry. Musicians like Limp Bizkit's Fred Durst and Chuck D from Public Enemy were singing Napster's praises. They all claimed that Shawn Fanning had brought the music world exactly what it needed.

Other musicians, however, weren't so happy with the arrangement that Fanning had set up. They felt that the fruits of their hard labor were being sucked away. Everyone from Hootie & the Blowfish to Dr. Dre took shots at Fanning and Napster.

But the most stunning and publicized attack came from a heavy metal band, Metallica. On April 13, 2000, roughly four months after the RIAA first filed court papers against Napster, Metallica filed its own suit

Metallica, Shawn's favorite band

against the upstart company. Furthermore, the band included Yale University, the University of Southern California, and Indiana University in its suit. Metallica was not only going after Napster, but also after the schools that, until this point, had allowed Napster to run on their networks.

This was a major turning point. First of all, Metallica has a rebellious reputation and was certainly a band that had the ear of America's youth. Its decision to go after Napster created a perception that Shawn Fanning might not actually be on the side of defiant young Americans, but might, in fact, be just another businessman trying to make a buck. Second, if Metallica actually won its suit, there would be no end to the lawsuits that would follow from other artists. The cash that Napster would have to shell out in damages would be endless, and the company would be finished. Just as important, if institutions like Yale and Indiana University lost in court, a whole new target would be established. Schools everywhere would shut Napster down for fear of getting dragged down with it. This led to the most profound implications of Metallica's accusations. It raised the question: Who is responsible for content on the Internet?

Until this point, Internet network managers were understood to be mere facilitators of communication. In other words, they kept the networks running but weren't responsible for how the networks were used. But Metallica's lawsuit held Internet providers accountable for content. If the courts ruled in Metallica's favor, there would be no end to the legal mess that would follow. Internet service providers from America Online to Yahoo! would have to rethink how they monitored the Internet.

Lars Ulrich, Metallica's drummer, talks to reporters about the band's lawsuit against Napster.

And there was one more issue—perhaps the biggest of all, from Shawn Fanning's point of view. Metallica was one of his favorite bands. He had even played Metallica songs in his high-school rock band. The implications of the suit were huge from a legal standpoint. But the implications were also huge from a personal perspective. Was this really the revolution that Fanning wanted to start? He had done all this because he loved music. Now one of his favorite bands was out to destroy him.

Bad Luck, Good Publicity

Court proceedings take time, especially when entire industries hang in the balance. The RIAA's suit was filed in December 1999. Metallica's followed in April 2000. Still, it would be months before a judge made any decision.

In the meantime, Napster was reaping huge benefits from the suit. Every time a musician got on TV to denounce Napster and its free music, new users would log on. Most people weren't horrified by the alleged copyright thefts of Shawn Fanning; instead they were thrilled by the ease with which they could download free music. Napster's user base was now more than twenty million, and growing by leaps and bounds.

Accompanying this was a shift in the kind of people using Napster. Before all the publicity, Napster had been used mostly by college kids and teenagers. Now, suddenly, people in their nineties were logging on. And they loved Napster every bit as much as college kids. Swing from the 1940s, blues from the 1920s, jazz from the 1960s—almost every kind of music was changing hands over Napster. Slowly the project that Shawn Fanning had started on the floor of his uncle's office was becoming an everyday part of people's lives—like a stereo or a television.

Still, for all the benefits of the publicity, the people at Napster knew the stakes were getting higher. No matter how many users they had, if a judge ruled they were violating copyrights, it was all over.

Big Changes

In an effort to smooth things over with Metallica and to make a show of good faith toward musicians in general, Fanning and Napster unexpectedly agreed to remove nearly three hundred thousand users from its site. These users had been identified by Metallica as people who had illegally traded Metallica songs. Some Napster supporters cried foul—the Web site seemed to be giving in too easily. But Napster wanted to show that it respected the wishes of the musicians whose works were flowing across the Web. This did not end the case, however, and Metallica pushed forward, claiming that removal of the user names was not enough.

Around the same time, Napster went through several other changes. First, the company managed to raise fifteen million dollars in new funding—essential money to keep the site going and to pay the lawyers. The cash came from an investment company called Hummer Winblad, cofounded by ex-basketball player John Hummer of the Seattle Supersonics. But Hummer Winblad contributed more than money. One of the firm's partners, Hank Barry, was named the new CEO of Napster, replacing Eileen Richardson. Richardson had been hired with the idea that her job would be temporary. Her talents were in starting up companies and raising money—skills for which a hard-nosed personality can be useful. But her aggressive style of management wasn't what was needed for Napster's new incarnation— and its new challenges. Napster needed more of a diplomat and peacemaker. As the court battle heated up, it seemed like a good time to switch management.

The other move Napster made was to hire David Boies. Boies had led the government's recent antitrust case against Microsoft. He knew the law surrounding copyrights and computers very well. And he was generally regarded as one of the most persuasive lawyers around. (His reputation was so good that he would be hired by Al Gore late in the fall of 2000 to manage the election difficulties in Florida surrounding Gore's campaign against George W. Bush.) Boies would take Shawn Fanning and his embattled Napster through the difficult court process—with luck, to victory.

Everyday Life

Throughout all the furor, Shawn Fanning's life in San Mateo remained much the same. He still wore his University of Michigan cap and baggy clothes. He still loved to play hoops and work out. He still ate pizza and cereal, although he experimented with a low-carbohydrate diet as part of his exercise routine. And he still stayed up all night writing code.

One difference was that Fanning had acquired a girlfriend—a fellow nineteen year old, whom he kept a secret from his buddies at Napster and the press. Another difference was that he treated himself to a reward for his hard work. He bought a Mazda RX7, a car he had long dreamed of owning.

Shawn Fanning was under huge pressure because of Napster's legal battles. But he was also making a point of relaxing a little more. With Boies and Barry on the Napster team, he didn't have to worry so much about the legal and business side of things. Napster was still facing lots of trouble. But Napster's employees now numbered around forty, they had acquired cool new offices in Redwood City, California (near San Mateo), and Fanning had hired experts to handle issues that were outside his own experience. Fanning was not a lawyer or an MBA, after all. He was a programmer.

Probably Fanning's most important role during the summer of 2000, and for the following year, was as the face and voice of Napster. Every day he became more and more of a hero to the millions of Napster users. He was a local celebrity and couldn't even go to the gym without being stopped or stared at. His face was on the cover of magazines like

BusinessWeek and *Fortune*. He was also getting good at speaking to the press about Napster, his hopes for the company, and its humble beginnings in Hull, Massachusetts. The more people heard his story, the more famous he became. Fanning wasn't just a great coder, a visionary, or a thoughtful businessman. He was a cool guy, too. People liked him. Kids identified with him. And people believed him when he said that he had built Napster simply because he loved music and the Internet and had a dream of combining the two.

CHAPTER FIVE

Napster Destroyed, Napster Reborn

The First Setback

Things began to get tougher in July 2000. After months of legal wrangling, a judge finally ruled on the case. The results were not good for Napster. On July 26, U.S. district judge Marilyn Patel ordered Napster to stop the trade of copyrighted songs over the Internet. She understood that Napster itself was not actually trading illegal MP3 files, but she held the company responsible because it had built the means to make the trades. As she said to a packed courtroom, "If you design a site . . . to enable infringement, you can't stand by and claim you don't know what's going on." She gave Napster two days to comply with her ruling.

The legal team, now headed by David Boies, sprang into action. They quickly held a press conference that was simulcast over the Web. In it Hank Barry and Shawn Fanning declared that the war was not over. "We will keep fighting for Napster and for your right to share music on the Internet," Shawn vowed. At the same time Boies filed a motion with the Ninth Circuit Court of Appeals.

Napster attorney David Boies takes questions after the court ruled against the company.

Just nine hours before Napster was supposed to shut down, the appeals court ordered Patel's verdict against Napster to be delayed while they looked over the case. It had been a nerve-racking week, but Napster had won another reprieve. Still, this was not the way Fanning's team had hoped that things would unfold. The fact that one judge had ruled against them meant that another might do the same. Fanning and Napster dug in their heels and waited, although it would again be a matter of months before the appeals judges would rule.

In the meantime Napster was still up and running. Millions more people were logging on, especially now that it looked as if the Web site might be shut down soon. People wanted to get what they could before the party was over. The name and reputation of Napster continued to grow.

Britney, Carson, and Shawn

As the appeals court began reviewing Judge Patel's decision, Shawn Fanning made a few deals with bands that had spoken out in favor of Napster. The most important connection was with the groups Limp Bizkit and Cypress Hill. Napster sponsored their free summer tour, and everywhere they went the Napster banner and the legend of Shawn Fanning followed.

The tour foreshadowed another moment in the spotlight for Fanning—one that would be talked about for months afterward. MTV decided to ask Fanning to be a presenter at the annual Music Video Awards. Next to the Grammys, it is the most important event of the year for the music industry, and MTV was going to showcase one of the most controversial people in the music business. Of course, MTV knew what it was doing. Record executives may have hated Fanning. Lots of musicians hated him, too. But fans loved him. And as he took his place onstage next to Carson Daly, the evening's master of ceremonies, the crowd went wild. Not only was

Shawn Fanning wore his Metallica T-shirt at the MTV Music Video Awards.

he the talk of the town at the time, but he walked out in front of the crowd and the cameras wearing a Metallica T-shirt. MTV cameras panned back and forth between Fanning and

Lars Ulrich (the drummer for Metallica and the man who had been leading the suit against Napster). Ulrich frowned. But at that moment Fanning was too busy to notice Ulrich's response. He had just been given the honor of introducing Britney Spears!

Fanning's next public appearance would be a little more serious. It was at about this time that the U.S. Senate Judiciary Committee asked to meet the creator of Napster. They had some questions they wanted to ask him.

Fred Durst of Limp Bizkit, one of Napster's allies in the music industry

The Trip to Provo

Part of Shawn Fanning's appeal was that he embodied the look and attitude of America's youth culture. He wore baggy clothes, loved swapping MP3s, and was irreverent when it came to big business telling him what to do. But another part of Fanning's appeal was that he just seemed so nice and unassuming. When he came before the Senate Judiciary Committee, this was again how he appeared. He got a haircut, dropped the messy clothes, put on a suit, and very humbly explained how Napster had come into the world.

The Senate Judiciary Committee was one of the most powerful bodies in Washington. It was a tough bunch of senators, who were used to making landmark decisions about the law. They were also not the type of people to be fooled by a suit and a new haircut. In fact, there was something slightly comical about watching the young man who had been vilified as the country's most dangerous Internet pirate politely describing his love for music. But there was also something compelling about his testimony. After listening to musicians and industry leaders, the committee was finally hearing from the person who had caused all the problems. And they discovered that they liked him.

The most important ally Shawn Fanning won that October 2000 was Orrin Hatch, the committee's chairman. Hatch certainly was not someone that people expected to side with Napster. He was a very powerful conservative Republican,

Utah senator Orrin Hatch was
Fanning's strongest ally on the
Senate Judiciary Committee.

who was frequently criticized by political pundits for being boring, straitlaced, and just plain mean. But Orrin Hatch was more complex than people had given him credit for. He was also a songwriter and a musician—a struggling one, as he claimed, and one who had little sympathy for the record industry. Hatch saw Napster in much the same way that Fanning did—as a music community that bypassed the control of powerful music executives. Hatch also claimed to have learned a lot from Napster. When he met with Metallica in an earlier hearing, he said he had just downloaded their music. He said it was "pretty darn good." This was something else Hatch and Fanning had in common. They both liked Metallica, even if Metallica disagreed with their opinions.

Officially, Hatch had no say in the court decision about Napster's legality. But Hatch was involved in writing new laws, and a court ruling was irrelevant if Congress changed the laws that the RIAA claimed Napster was violating. Hatch's sympathy made it clear that if Napster lost in court, there were other ways for it to stay alive. Almost as important, Hatch's support demonstrated very clearly that Napster was not just for rebellious college kids and petty thieves. A powerful senator saw the value of Napster and understood that the more than thirty million users of the site constituted a political force to be reckoned with. Fanning could not have found a better endorsement.

New Allies

By the end of October, a month after Fanning's meeting with the Judiciary Committee, Napster earned another important ally and business partner. In a deal that stunned the music business, Fanning and his company joined forces with a large German firm called Bertelsmann. Among its many holdings,

Bertelsmann is one of the biggest record companies in the world.

Bertelsmann agreed to withdraw its support from the RIAA lawsuit, provide financial assistance to Napster, and permit Napster to trade its huge inventory of copyrighted songs across the Internet. In exchange Bertelsmann would acquire a major share of Napster. People quickly scrambled to understand this new relationship. Did it mean the record industry was giving in or that the rebels were selling out?

By most estimates, this partnership meant neither. It really represented a natural step in the debate over Internet music. Record companies had to accept that the traditional system of music distribution—CDs on sale at a store—was on its way out. The companies could either be on board or be undermined by the new technology. As for Napster, it had to start making money. The company had heavy legal fees to pay. And it was a business, after all. Its goal had always been to make a profit eventually.

The plan was to charge a subscription fee for Napster. It would no longer be free. Still, it would be quite inexpensive. Most people predicted a subscription price of between two and six dollars per month. For that, users would be able to download anything from Bertelsmann's huge song library. And because Bertelsmann owned the copyright, there would be no lawsuits claiming theft.

The long-term plan was eventually to offer the service to other record companies. The Napster-Bertelsmann model included plans for special software that would track what songs were exchanged. Every time someone downloaded a song, Napster would pay the song's copyright holder a small fee, so any record company or musician could make money through Napster. According to Napster and Bertelsmann, this would allow everyone to be fairly compensated while providing a great, cheap service to Napster's members.

Of course, this deal was a hedge against the impending decision from the Ninth Circuit Court of Appeals. If Napster won the appeal, all bets were off. Users could continue to share music for free, without violating copyrights. The fee structure would be scrapped or redeveloped. By this point, however, members of the Napster camp knew there was a strong chance they would lose in court.

A Verdict

Fall ended and winter came as people waited expectantly for the judges to decide the fate of Napster. The Bertelsmann-Napster deal was announced on October 31, 2000. For months afterward experts were predicting that a court ruling would come "any day," but it was not until mid-February that a verdict finally came down.

For Napster the news was bad. The company had lost its appeal and was ordered to halt the swapping of copyrighted music across their server. This time the ruling would stand.

Napster had planned for this verdict. Some on the Napster team had even expected it. The company immediately set to work on

Shawn Fanning and Napster CEO Hank Barry try to look upbeat after losing their legal appeal.

the subscription system, intending to go back online with Bertelsmann's song library (and soon, they hoped, the song libraries of other record companies) as soon as the software was ready. Still, whatever form Napster would take in the future, the version that Shawn Fanning had developed on the floor of his uncle's office in Hull, Massachusetts, was gone.

A New Plan

There was still hope that Congress might act. New laws could restore Napster to its former state. But because of the Bertelsmann deal, this was looking increasingly unlikely. Senator Hatch's support for Napster still menaced the RIAA, but he had also made it clear that he preferred the two sides to come to their own resolution rather than have the government interfere.

Napster's first priority now was to obey the court order and prevent copyrighted songs from streaming through its site. With the new business model and subscription plan in development, Napster was hoping that the limitations on its selection of offerings would only be temporary. But until the new plan was implemented, Napster was severely limited.

Imitating the Bertelsmann-Napster subscription plan, other major record labels began announcing their plans for similar systems. The very companies that had shut Napster down were now working on peer-to-peer software. They would allow their own copyrighted music to be swapped on-line and, like the new Napster, would charge subscription rates for the service. This would mean serious competition for Fanning. If other record companies could build their own Web sites, they might not let Napster users swap their songs— even for a fee.

In addition, during Napster's long battle Napster clones like Gnutella and IMesh had also popped up. These sites were similar to Napster except that they existed entirely on the Web and had no central server that did the indexing. That meant that even if their programs were illegal, they would be almost impossible to stop. This was going to prove to be another headache for the music industry, but it was a battle for a different day.

So in the end, what was Napster left with? Many believe that the company wound up with nothing. Others say Napster had already created four of the most important elements of a powerful business. First, the Napster name was known by virtually everyone. It was a compelling brand name, like Sony or Coke, and would draw people to the site. Second, Napster had a loyal user base. People who had used Napster before would probably use it again rather than switch to a different provider. Third, the company had finally figured out how to make money. By charging a subscription fee, Napster was moving from being a great idea to being a great business. Finally, Napster had Shawn Fanning, who was not only a great programmer, but also a celebrity. If there was ever a Tiger Woods of the Internet—a character that people not only recognized but loved—it was Shawn Fanning. As long as he was on the Napster and Bertelsmann team, he would draw business. For all the deals he had made in the previous year, he was still the scruffy, rebellious kid from Cape Cod who gave everyone free music. The right to be a part of Fanning's story just might be the most important asset Napster and Bertelsmann own.

Napster's Future, Napster's Legacy

Without question, Shawn Fanning lost something when the Ninth Circuit judges rejected Napster's appeal. But he also found himself with new opportunities and a reputation that guaranteed he would have influence in the world of computers and the Internet for a long time to come. He was only twenty years old, and he had taken on one of the biggest industries in America—and very nearly won. Better still, the vision he had for the Internet's potential was fulfilled. Even if it didn't take the form he had originally intended, Napster and the entire music industry would bear his stamp . . . at least until the next-best thing came along.

But perhaps even more important, this kid from Harwich, Massachusetts, had changed the Internet itself. While people were wrangling over copyright laws, thousands of programmers were exploring the potential uses of peer-to-peer software. With people opening up their personal hard drives to each other in this new way, Fanning had created something much bigger than a community of music lovers.

Thanks to the model he created, cancer institutes are now dividing up work across personal hard drives to process medical data that are too vast for even the fastest supercomputers. Astronomers are downloading complicated data to people's personal hard drives for evaluation of "cosmic noise" that might point to signs of alien life in the universe. The Human Genome Project created a version of peer-to-peer software to store and access the information it had collected on human DNA.

All these scientists had long been looking for a way to handle the vast amounts of data they gathered. The peer-to-peer model was a perfect solution. Thus, while the music industry continued to fight over how to divide up profits, peer-to-peer software was already being used in new and innovative ways.

The world today knows Shawn Fanning as the kid who gave us free music and wore the Metallica T-shirt on MTV. He is also known as the rebellious young upstart who won the support of Senator Orrin Hatch. His place in history, however, will be as the man who changed the Internet forever.

sources and bibliography

Articles

Fredman, Nathaniel. "Shawn Fanning: Napster Founder and Former NU Student." *The Northeastern News*. October 18, 2000.

Milton, Susan. "Creator of Internet Software Sends Shock Waves Through Music Industry." *Cape Cod Times*. March 1, 2000.

Sheffield, Rob. "People of the Year: Shawn Fanning of Napster." *Rolling Stone*. December 14, 2000.

Stern, Christopher. "Hill Takes Notice of Napster Legal Fray." *The Washington Post*. February 16, 2001.

Web sites

Ante, Spencer E. "Napster's Shawn Fanning: The Teen Who Woke Up Web Music." www.Businessweek.com. April 13, 2000.

Cohen, Adam. "Taps for Napster?" www.Time.com. July 31, 2000.

Greenfeld, Karl Taro. "Meet the Napster." www.Time.com. October 2, 2000.

Pellegrini, Frank. "Napster Turns Orrin Hatch into One Groovy Cat." www.Time.com. July 11, 2000.

Pellegrini, Frank. "BMG and Napster: If You Can't Beat 'Em Buy 'Em." www.Time.com. November 6, 2000.

Taylor, Chris and Frank Pellegrini. "The End of Napster as We Know It." www.Time.com. March 3, 2001.

"Testimony of Shawn Fanning Before the Senate Judiciary Committee, Provo Utah." Napster Online Pressroom. October 9, 2000.

Photography credits

index

Page numbers in *italics* refer to illustrations.